WESSEX MURDER STORIES

A SELECTION OF SOLVED AND UNSOLVED MURDERS FROM
AROUND DORSET, HAMPSHIRE AND WILTSHIRE

Neil Walden

BRADWELL
BOOKS

Published by Bradwell Books

11 Orgreave Close Sheffield S13 9NP

Email: books@bradwellbooks.co.uk

British Library Cataloguing in Publication Data: a catalogue record for this book is available from the British Library.

1st Edition

ISBN: 9781912060610

Design by: Andy Caffrey

Typeset by: Mark Titterton

Photograph credits: The author, Creative Commons (CC) and indicated separately

Print: Gomer Press, Llandysul, Ceredigion SA44 4JL

CONTENTS

1.	THE ROADSIDE MURDER MYSTERY	6
2.	THE BOURNEMOUTH CLIFF TRAGEDY	12
3.	THE DEVIZES MURDER CASE	19
4.	THE WORTHY MURDER	23
5.	MURDER IN A WOOD	27
6.	THE SWINDON BAR TRAGEDY	31
7.	THE VILLA MURDER	35
8.	THE BASINGSTOKE CORNFIELD TRAGEDY	40
9.	THE MELKSHAM MURDER	43
10.	THE SALISBURY HORROR	47
11.	THE GUSSAGE MURDER	53
12.	THE MURDER AT BROADWINDSOR	58
13.	THE FORDINGBRIDGE MURDER	63
14.	DEATH OF A DORSET COWMAN	67
15.	THE SWINDON WIDOW'S MURDER	72
16.	THE CHINE MURDER	75

INTRODUCTION

ALL OF THE TRUE MURDER STORIES TO BE FOUND IN THIS BOOK
COME FROM THE WESSEX AREA OF ENGLAND, WHICH COVERS
DORSET, HAMPSHIRE AND WILTSHIRE.

Even the most recent story from this collection is now
over seventy years old, and yet these cases continue to
fascinate us. For example, when I worked in Salisbury
the story of Teddy Haskell was still talked about. As
well as books written about the case there was even
an excellent recreation of the murder trial staged in the
Guildhall.

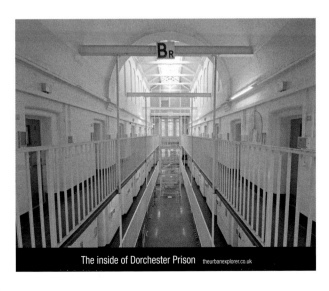

The inside of Dorchester Prison theurbanexplorer.co.uk

At the time of writing there is great interest in the closure of Dorchester Prison with the belief that the redevelopment will surely lead to the discovery of the body of Martha Brown. Martha's story (the murder at Broadwinsor) is the earliest in this book and her execution was famously attended by Thomas Hardy. Of course it is the novels of Hardy that have done so much to establish the modern notion of Wessex.

The title of each of the chapters is taken from the newspaper reports of the time. Where the stories are particularly well known, such as that of Heath or Toplis, I have tried to reference the case against local landmarks that can still be seen today. You will also find other cases that may be less well known but still provide a fascinating insight into human nature.

The Roadside Murder Mystery

IN JUNE 1920, WHEN PERCY TOPLIS WAS SHOT DEAD IN PENRITH, IT WAS THE FINAL ACT IN A DRAMA THAT HAD STARTED SIX WEEKS EARLIER AND 300 MILES AWAY IN SALISBURY, WITH THE MURDER OF A TAXI DRIVER.

Sidney Spicer lived in London Road in Salisbury. He had originally been a farmer and, having lost all of the fingers on one hand, had been unable to serve in the Great War. Most recently he had been driving a taxi in the local area.

Witnesses on the night of the murder say that a man dressed as a sergeant-major came out of the hedge and had a conversation with Spicer. It seems that the soldier wanted to hire the cab to take him from Amesbury to Andover. Spicer said that he was currently engaged on another job and couldn't take him, but that he would return in a quarter of an hour. Spicer then took his existing passengers to Bulford.

Another witness, Edward Heather, places Spicer at the Rose and Crown in Salisbury at 9pm. Spicer had just dropped off his passengers and told Heather that he had a job waiting for him, but that he was now short of fuel. Heather, who was a fellow taxi driver, arranged for Spicer to be loaned a tin of petrol before he went on his way to pick up his final customer.

The following morning the doctor stated that Sidney Spicer had been shot from behind with no signs of a struggle. It seems that the body must have been dragged some distance while face downwards as his waistcoat was covered in mud and more mud was found in his mouth. In addition to the car being missing, Spicer had been robbed of some of his personal possessions. He was known to have had approximately £15 on him, but there was no sign of this money, nor did he have his gold watch or driving licence, which were known to have been on him.

The murderer was Percy Toplis from Alfreton in Derbyshire. Although still only 23 years of age, he was already a habitual criminal. In 1908 in Chesterfield he was convicted of stealing newspapers and, soon after this, of stealing two railway tickets (at this time he was using the assumed name of Francis Edmundson). His crimes were escalating in severity and, under the guise of being William Denison, he was charged with stealing a purse. Then, in February 1912, he pleaded guilty to the charge of attempted rape and was given a sentence of two years' hard labour.

Percy Toplis, the murderer of Sidney Spicer © Bill Walden

On his release from Lincoln Prison, Toplis volunteered for the Royal Army Medical Corps. In recent years a story has been circulated that he took part in a revolt of soldiers at a training camp. It was an event that soon spiralled out of control. It certainly sounds like the sort of thing that he might have been involved with and the story is clearly the reason that in some quarters Toplis became known as 'The Monocled Mutineer', but it remains contentious as to whether or not he was actually present at that time.

After briefly serving in Egypt and India Toplis found that his health was starting to suffer. He was hospitalised for dysentery and he also contracted malaria. Recovering back in England he revived his interest in adopting different aliases, particularly that of an army captain, and he was sentenced at Nottingham Assizes to two years in prison for fraud. By 1920, free once more, Toplis had managed to join the Royal Army Service Corps, and was stationed in Wiltshire.

The first thing that Toplis did after the killing of Spicer was to drive the car back to his army camp. In the cookhouse he struck up a conversation with a fellow soldier, Private Henry Fellowes, an impressionable nineteen-year-old, and before long he was inviting him to go for ride in a motor car that he had recently come by. The pair got as far as Marlborough before stopping so that Toplis could go into the woods to burn some clothes which had been worn at the murder scene. After that there was a stop at Cirencester owing to engine trouble and a mechanic was summoned to fix it. Throughout, Toplis remained morose and hardly spoke a word to Fellowes.

They stopped off at a garage in Gloucester on the Sunday morning for more petrol. Here the two men inadvertently left a clue in the form of an empty petrol can on which there were traces of blood. But by the time that the garage owner had informed the police, the fugitives were well on their way to Wales.

The two men stayed overnight in the Grosvenor Hotel, which was considered to be one of the better hotels in Swansea. The next morning Toplis read in the newspapers that Spicer's body had been found – by a blacksmith cycling to work – and that they were wanted men. Perturbed that the crime had been so rapidly discovered they drove to Swansea Bay station and abandoned Spicer's car.

Running low on ideas, Percy Toplis said that he was off to London while his young accomplice simply decided to return to the army camp where, on arrival, he was incarcerated for being absent without leave. In no time at all he was relating the story of the trip to Wales although stressing that he had no involvement in the murder of Sidney Spicer.

Now a wanted man, Toplis probably spent the next couple of weeks in London posing, once again, as an army officer. Before long the newspapers started to link Toplis to recent attacks on other taxi drivers and this soon escalated. Toplis was connected to a number of other murders including that of Nurse Shore on a train in Sussex, Nellie Rault, who was a young girl murdered in Bedford, Reuben Mort, an old man killed in Bolton and just about any other unsolved case of recent times. In reality there was no evidence to link him to any murder apart from that of the Salisbury taxi driver.

Toplis soon left London and zigzagged all over the British Isles in a fairly random way. Regular sightings acted to fuel the legend and added to the feeling that he might turn up anywhere. On 1 June a farmer in northern Scotland alerted the police to a possible sighting. When they investigated, Toplis fired his pistol, wounding two men and escaping the scene on a bicycle. His next port of call was Carlisle. After acting suspiciously he was questioned by the police but was able to brazen it out. However, after his release the local police realised that the man must have been Toplis.

The events were reaching their inevitable conclusion. In the knowledge that he had a gun, and positive that he would resist arrest, an ambush involving armed police was arranged. Percy Toplis, the murderer of the Salisbury taxi driver Sidney Spicer, was gunned down in Penrith on 6 June 1920.

PENRITH CIVIC SOCIETY

PERCY TOPLIS
known as the
Monocled Mutineer,
shot and killed here whilst
on the run for murder
6th June 1920

Plaque marking the site of the shooting of Toplis

The Bournemouth Cliff Tragedy

ON 20 FEBRUARY 1908 THE BODY OF A WOMAN WAS FOUND ON THE CLIFFS AT SOUTHBOURNE, IN BOURNEMOUTH. SHE HAD BEEN BEATEN TO DEATH WITH A BLUNT WEAPON.

The dead woman was soon identified as Emma Sherriff, a 36-year-old dressmaker who had been living at Tower House, 80 Palmerston Road in Boscombe. She had not been seen for the previous two days. Quickly suspicion fell on one particular friend of Emma's.

Frank McGuire was tall, with a striking appearance, and was fifteen years younger than Emma. In 1901 he had joined the Royal Horse and Field Artillery. In those early years he regularly visited Emma, of whom he had grown fond, and who was living conveniently close to his own mother. But then Frank disappeared.

After 18 months Frank McGuire suddenly resurfaced. He resumed correspondence and, knowing that he was forgiven by Emma for his sudden departure, he arrived back in Boscombe in early February 1908. McGuire stayed in another flat at Emma's apartment block for ten days in total and once again Frank and Emma seemed devoted to one another.

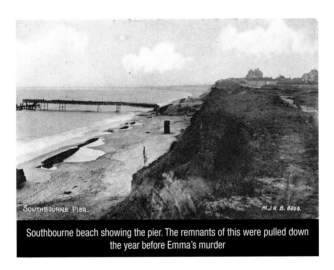

SOUTHBOURNE PIER.

Southbourne beach showing the pier. The remnants of this were pulled down the year before Emma's murder

In the early afternoon of Monday 17 February Frank left on the train to Waterloo to carry out some business in London. He was due to return the same evening and meet up with Emma again. While he was away Emma had a chance to reflect on recent events – and she also noticed that some of her prize items of jewellery were missing. There followed a strange period, which was to be the last day of Emma's life, during which telegrams and letters were sent and received, and Emma is reported as being very upset. A friend reported that Emma did duly confront Frank about the missing jewellery but that he simply said that he had taken it only to tease her, and intended to return it later. However, it was at this point that Emma herself disappeared.

When Emma's body was found the police went to Frank's London address to arrest him. At this point he insisted that he had not been in Bournemouth at the time of the murder. His mother was able to produce a letter from Frank, which had been posted in London at 8.30pm the previous evening and which seemed to offer an alibi.

With investigations under way into Frank's involvement in the case, startling evidence regarding the missing period of his life emerged. It seems that he had deserted from the army and had been taken under the wing of a retired officer. William Frederick Powell Moore was the son of a successful architect and a Major in the East Kent Regiment. It seems to have been an odd relationship between Powell and Frank, with the major apparently treating the younger man as his son. Frank had even used the name of Powell as one of his aliases. It is easy to imagine that Moore had been an elderly man whom McGuire simply took advantage of, but that doesn't seem to be the case. In fact they appear to have been rather a good match. The Major resigned his commission in the army in 1885 and simultaneously left his wife of seven years in a case that made news at the time: as she was seeing him off at Folkestone harbour to go on business he simply announced that he was never coming back. It became a celebrated divorce case when the marriage was dissolved the following year.

At the time of Emma's murder Powell was said by Frank to be living in Leicester, but in reality he was in prison. The Major had just received a four-month sentence for obtaining money by false pretences and absconding from a Bristol hotel without paying a £17 bill. It seems that with the Major in prison, his protégé had come up with a new scheme, for it was at this time that Frank had resurfaced in Emma's life with such terrible consequences.

Another of Frank McGuire's aliases was Hayman. It was a name stolen from another hitherto unknown area of his life. Henry Hayman was a Rochester-based painter, and Frank was engaged to be married to his daughter. He was also acting as Hayman's agent by selling paintings to galleries on his behalf. Clearly that business was not going well and Frank was heavily in debt.

When McGuire's London home was investigated by the police they found a number of pawn tickets associated with jewellery stolen from his fiancée. Things were looking bleak for Frank, who was now charged with the murder of Emma Sherriff.

The trial commenced at Winchester Castle on 28 May 1908. The prosecution was armed with an expert knowledge of the railway timetable and was able to show how Frank could have travelled back and forth between London and Bournemouth and successfully committed the murder within the necessary timeframe. One problem for the prosecution was the 8.30 letter from London but that was explained by the evidence of a shoeshine boy who had been given sixpence for posting the letter on the proviso he did not do so until after 8pm.

Some of the evidence was related to Emma's handbag and a few other personal items which were things that she would always carry about with her but puzzlingly were not found by the body. The items were found back at Emma's house but left in slightly improbable places. It was asserted that Frank had taken these items at first and then, fearful of them being traced to him, decided to put them back in the flat without knowing their correct places.

McGuire was impressive in his account of the days surrounding the murder. He seemed to have explanations for most of the anomalies in his case. For example, the business with the letter was because he did not want his mother to know that he had gone back to Bournemouth, and any witness who claimed to have seen him on the day of the murder (and there was at least one of these) was mistaken as he stated that he had not been in Bournemouth or seen Emma.

It was at the end of the third day of the trial that the jury retired to consider their verdict. They surfaced once to say that they were split in their decision and were sent back to see if they could reach a unanimous decision. By 11pm that night they admitted that they could not all agree on a verdict. There was going to have to be a retrial.

After a further tantalising three weeks the Attorney General decided to drop the charges against McGuire and it was announced that he was to be released. On reflection the prosecution had realised that it would be almost impossible to secure a conviction. Frank now stated his intention to set up a picture business (along the lines of the one that had done so poorly in his guise as Frank Hayman), but before there could be any question of starting a new life he needed to account for his desertion from the ranks. In July 1908 he was rearrested.

Following his court martial McGuire spent 84 days in a military prison in Aldershot for desertion. On his release he headed off to Mundesley in Norfolk. He stayed there until the March of 1909 when once again he was in trouble, this time for the non-payment of rent for the cottage he was sharing with his girlfriend (they were living as Captain and Mrs Francis). He made a run for it London but was arrested for travelling on a train without a ticket.

In July 1910 McGuire received a sentence of three months in prison for obtaining money under false pretences from a book company and at the time of 1911 census he was once again in prison in Portsmouth. In 1914 he was in Wormwood Scrubs with his release date due at the end of January 1915. From that point onwards, with McGuire using a series of aliases (such as Robert Arthur Tresham and Francis Tempest) he becomes increasingly difficult to trace. Meanwhile the murder of Emma Sherriff remains officially unsolved.

The Devizes Murder Case

EDWARD HAMPTON HAD ALREADY EXPERIENCED ONE TRAGEDY IN THE FAMILY WHEN HIS DAUGHTER WAS CHARGED WITH MANSLAUGHTER. THE JUDGE PARTICULARLY HIGHLIGHTED EDWARD'S CRUELTY IN FAILING TO OFFER ANY HELP. DECIDING TO BE MORE CHARITABLE THE NEXT TIME THAT SOMEONE CAME TO HIM LOOKING FOR SANCTUARY, HE SOON ALLOWED A MURDERER INTO HIS HOUSE.

Edward was born in 1838 and his sister Emily seven years later. They lived at various addresses in Rowde and Devizes. Processing tobacco and snuff would have been a significant industry in Devizes at this time, and we still have Snuff Street leading off the Market Place in Devizes as a reminder of those times. The Hamptons were a family of tobacco cutters and, once old enough, Edward was soon working in a tobacconist's shop.

When Edward's wife died in 1881 Emily moved back in with her brother at his house in Avon Terrace, where she assisted by looking after the children and working as Edward's housekeeper. The previous year Emily had married Benjamin Purnell, a porter at the workhouse in Devizes where they were both working. Like her brother, Benjamin had been born in 1838 and for some years he had served in the army, belonging to the 62nd (Wiltshire) Regiment of Foot.

The relationship between Benjamin and Emily was a fiery one and the marriage got off to a very poor start. After six weeks of married life Benjamin grew tired of Emily's continual nagging and promptly disappeared for five years. He made a brief reappearance before vanishing once again.

While Purnell was away, in the November of 1887, Edward Hampton's daughter Rhoda was charged with manslaughter. This followed the death of her newly born child who had died from exposure and neglect. At Rhoda's trial, in which ultimately the case against her was dramatically dropped, Edward had come out particularly badly. He was portrayed as having heartlessly turned his daughter out into the streets, telling her to go to the workhouse.

In 1889, nine years after his marriage to Emily, Benjamin suddenly returned to the area. He found a labouring job and he too moved into Edward's home in Avon Terrace. The house was small and in no time the relationship between the Purnells became strained once again. At least part of this friction concerned Benjamin's doubts that he was the father of Emily's young daughter. He

Avon Terrace in Devizes, beside the Kennet and Avon Canal

may have had a point, as Benjamin's appearances in Devizes had been erratic and would have offered a fairly narrow window of opportunity in which to father a child.

After a particularly violent argument in the early hours of 9 November 1889, regarding Emily supposedly wasting money on a new petticoat, Benjamin murdered his wife. The argument had started the previous night and, while there were no other adults in the house, it was clearly heard by the children and was still raging away downstairs at six the next morning. The dispute came to a sudden conclusion. When Edward's son came down to check on his aunt and uncle, at first only Benjamin could be found. Emily was in fact a few yards from the house in the back yard and was mortally wounded from a series of blows to the head with a hatchet. A neighbour was roused who, in turn, summoned a doctor. Emily was now taken on a stretcher to the cottage hospital in Devizes.

The police soon arrived at the house but Benjamin was nowhere to be seen. He must have realised that there was no hope of evading justice and had decided to walk into town to hand himself in at the police station. He had no hesitation in admitting that he was responsible for the act and showed no sign of remorse or concern for Emily. At this point Emily was still alive, although she had received five fractures to the head and never regained consciousness. She died the following day.

The trial of Benjamin Purnell commenced in Devizes on 23 November 1889. As Purnell had no means to afford a defence counsel he had one appointed for him. It started with a fairly rudimentary error as, when asked if he was pleading guilty to the charge of murder, Benjamin confirmed that he was. It took a quick consultation with his surprised counsel to clarify the fact that he did in fact want to claim his innocence.

In the end there was not a great deal that could be offered in evidence by the defence. Even if there was some doubt regarding the paternity of their child, it was never going to be an excuse for murder. Benjamin Purnell was found guilty and he was executed at Devizes Gaol on 9 December 1889.

The Cart and Horses in Kings Worthy where the inquest was held

people were brought forward, each of whom had seen the two men walking back towards London. Just about every one of these travellers had in turn been asked by the two boys whether they were heading in the right direction for London.

On 7 April it seems that James and Albert had enjoyed a drink together in the Hyde Tavern in Winchester. Then soon afterwards a resident of nearby Worthy Toll Bar Cottages sighted the two of them close to the field where the body was found. A witness named Ben Smith gave evidence that he had seen Brown leaving the field on the morning of the 8th, but this time he was alone.

The post-mortem examination of Parker revealed that he had been battered around the head prior to having his throat slit. The coroner's jury had no hesitation in concluding that James Parker had been wilfully murdered by Brown, who was now sent for trial at Winchester Assizes.

At the trial Brown stuck to his original explanation that he and Parker had split up on good terms in Winchester. They had gone their separate ways as he had wanted to catch the train while Parker had wanted to continue the journey on foot. Brown was insistent that all the witnesses must be mistaken. The defence pointed out that although there was a mass of evidence against Brown it was all circumstantial. There appeared to be a lack of malice, premeditation or a particularly compelling motive.

The jury took two and a half hours to come to their verdict. Brown was sentenced to hang at Winchester prison. Two days after the trial, he finally provided details about the attack and confessed to murder. It seems that the only motive was robbery. Parker had just a few shillings left from his week's wages and it was for this that Brown had killed his friend. With no hope of a reprieve, he now directed the police back to the vicinity of the field where the murder took place and to the hiding place of the razor and hammer that he had used in the attack. Albert Brown was executed on 31 May 1886.

Murder in a Wood

ON 11 JULY 1917 THE BODY OF VERA GLASSPOOL WAS FOUND IN THE WOODS AT LONGWOOD NEAR WINCHESTER. DESPITE THERE BEING SEVERAL SUSPECTS, AND EVEN ONE CONFESSION, THE CASE REMAINS UNSOLVED.

Vera was born in 1902 and lived at Rose Cottage in Baybridge. She was the second youngest child of a large family. At 14 years of age she started work at Longwood House as a scullery maid. Although Vera lived up at the big house, she would always visit her family home for a couple of afternoons a week when work permitted. On Tuesday 10 July she left Longwood House to walk to Baybridge.

It was Vera's 28-year-old married sister, Edith Morris, out with her father looking for Vera, who was to find the body in an area known as Featherbed Copse. At the initial inquest two days later, Edith described how they found Vera about 35 yards from the road with a wound on her throat and blood on her mackintosh. She also described how other items of Vera's clothing were 'disarranged'.

Dr Richards examined the body and said that death was partly due to strangulation (using the right sleeve of her raincoat) as well as a stab wound to her neck which had probably been inflicted while she was semi-conscious. It was also concluded that it would have been impossible for Vera to have inflicted the injuries on herself. Vera was not carrying any money with her, as this was always handed directly over to her parents, but it was believed that her watch was now missing.

A second inquest was to be held at the Memorial Hall in Owslebury on 19 July and a verdict of unlawful murder was announced. Although some seemed to think that the murderer might be someone accustomed to the slaughter of animals, this was just conjecture. The fact remained that the army camp at Hazeley Down was just one and a half miles away and suspicion was always likely to centre there.

Evidence was given that Vera had told a fellow servant that she had arranged to meet some soldiers on the afternoon of 10 July. Florence Wells, a housemaid at Longwood House, told the inquest that she and Vera had met up with a couple of soldiers on the Sunday before Vera's death. She said that they had made further arrangements for a future rendezvous but she added, rather ominously, that Vera had subsequently told her that she had made her own separate arrangements to meet two soldiers from the camp. On the day of the murder Vera was not seen in the company of any of the soldiers and the last sighting of her was by the wife of

The long-demolished Longwood House near Owslebury where Vera lived

a gardener from Longwood. This witness said that she had seen Vera walking alone past her house before disappearing around the corner.

Since that time there have been several theories put forward as to who was responsible for this attack on Vera. In particular there is talk of a link to the murder of Emily Trigg in Kent the previous year. Emily was a twenty-year-old maid from Rochester who was meeting with soldiers based near her home and was, it seems, murdered in a similar manner to Vera. A soldier was arrested in connection with this murder but was released when no evidence was offered against him. It is an intriguing theory that this man may have been one of the soldiers that Vera was due to meet near the camp where he was subsequently based. After Vera's death there were no further murders of this type and this suspect soon returned to war, where he died in action later that year.

Another soldier, Private William Fenn of the Medical Corps, did confess to the murder of Vera Glasspool, however. He was arrested in Blackpool and there was a flurry of activity, although the subsequent enquiries proved that he was in a camp many miles away at the time of Vera's murder and so the charges were dropped.

A sum of £50 was offered for further information relating to Vera's death but the reward remained unclaimed. The trail went cold and the case abruptly disappeared from the newspapers to make way for news of the ongoing war.

The Swindon Bar Tragedy

ALTHOUGH ONLY NINETEEN YEARS OF AGE, ESTHER SWINFORD HAD ALREADY BEEN WORKING AS A DOMESTIC SERVANT AT THE SHIP INN AT WESTCOTT PLACE FOR TWO YEARS. ON 18 SEPTEMBER 1903 A MAN WALKED INTO THE BAR AND ORDERED A BOTTLE OF BEER. HE THEN PROMPTLY PULLED A GUN FROM HIS POCKET AND SHOT HER DEAD.

Esther was originally from Gloucestershire, where her father was a farm labourer. She was already a 'live-in' servant at the Ship when she first met Edward Richard Palmer and the couple became engaged in 1902. With the wedding date set, Esther discovered that the hard-earned cash she had been giving to Palmer towards their future together had been frittered away.

Now, unconvinced of Edward's commitment, Esther broke off the engagement and her ex-fiancé left Swindon. Palmer supposedly made a trip to Canada at this time, but there is little evidence to support this claim. It seems more likely that his travels took him no further than Reading, where he found a job as a gardener.

The Ship in Westcott Street at about the time of the murder cc

Soon Palmer returned to Swindon seeking employment at the Great Western Railway works. It was where he had worked once before but he was unable to secure employment here on this second occasion. It was soon after this that Palmer came back to the Ship Inn and shot Esther dead with a single bullet to the heart.

Palmer's explanation for the shooting was that while Esther was fetching the cigar that he had ordered he had taken out a revolver in the hope of giving her a scare. Esther then supposedly grabbed him by the wrist, which caused the gun to accidentally go off. When the landlord came to see what had happened, Palmer, who was covering his face with his hands, said, 'All right,

Contemporary picture of Palmer from the time of his trial cc

I done it,' which seems an unusual turn of phrase for someone who had just accidentally killed his former fiancée.

Palmer appeared at Wiltshire Assizes on 28 October 1903 charged with Esther's wilful murder. He soon confirmed that he was in the habit of carrying a revolver but reiterated that he had only intended to frighten Esther. Apparently he was annoyed that she had not spoken to him. A circular photograph of Esther with the words 'the curse of my life' written in pencil in the white border was found on Palmer after his arrest. When questioned about the photograph Palmer seemed unable to give any evidence or explanation as to why he had written on it.

Palmer's former employers described him as a steady and hard-working man, and a medical report from his own doctor confirmed his mental state as quite normal. The court heard how, before leaving town, Palmer had confided in a neighbour that he had recently been told something about his fiancée and as a result he would never marry her, hinting at some impropriety. There seems no evidence for this and it was an accusation that the prosecution firmly refuted. Palmer's defence counsel pleaded for an acquittal, calling for a verdict of accidental death or manslaughter. However, it took the jury just half an hour to return a guilty verdict.

As Palmer awaited his execution at Devizes Prison, set for 17 November 1903, he said that he felt nothing but regret and repentance for his actions on what he referred to as 'that mad day'.

The Villa Murder

IN DECEMBER 1923, 56-YEAR-OLD FRANCIS RATTENBURY MET AND FELL IN LOVE WITH ALMA PAKENHAM, A DIVORCEE HALF HIS AGE. RATTENBURY WAS MARRIED WITH TWO CHILDREN AND, FOLLOWING AN ACRIMONIOUS DIVORCE, HE SET UP HOME WITH ALMA IN MANOR ROAD ON BOURNEMOUTH'S EAST CLIFF. IT WAS HERE, TWELVE YEARS LATER, THAT RATTENBURY WAS TO BE THE VICTIM IN ONE OF THE MOST FAMOUS MURDER CASES THIS COUNTRY HAS EVER KNOWN.

Rattenbury was originally from Yorkshire and, having learned his craft as an architect at his uncle's practice in Bradford, he embarked on an illustrious career in Canada, where his work included the Law Courts in Vancouver and the Parliament Buildings in British Columbia.

Francis Rattenbury is now more remembered for being a murder victim than as a talented architect CC

Alma was Canadian by birth and an accomplished pianist and songwriter. She moved to England with her first husband, although he was to die in the Battle of the Somme. Alma also served in the Great War as part of an ambulance unit working behind the French lines and she had been decorated for her bravery. At the end of the war, she married Captain Pakenham and moved with him to America. Following the break-up of this second marriage Alma and her young son joined her mother in Vancouver. Alma returned to playing music and one day, after a recital in Victoria, she had her first fateful meeting with her husband-to-be.

By September 1934, Francis Rattenbury, with his best years as an architect long behind him, was living with Alma and their children at 5 Manor Road on Bournemouth's East Cliff, a house that was also known as the Villa Madeira. It was here that eighteen-year-old George Stoner came to be interviewed for the position of chauffeur-handyman in response to an advertisement placed in the *Bournemouth Daily Echo*.

Stoner had been raised in Bournemouth, splitting his time between the family home in Redhill and his grandparents' house in Ensbury Park. After starting work at the Villa he became a permanent resident. By this time Francis Rattenbury was drinking heavily, and he was often said to be depressed and suicidal and not interested in what Alma got up to. The lack of interest extended to the fact that soon his wife was clearly having an affair with Stoner.

Matters came to a head on the afternoon of 24 March 1935. Stoner was agitated about a prospective trip that Alma and her husband were taking to visit a friend in Bridport. Stoner had become increasingly possessive of Alma and did not want her to go. Ominously he now borrowed a wooden mallet from his grandparents in Ensbury Park, telling them it was to erect a screen in the garden.

Later that evening, Stoner came to find Alma and told her that he had hurt Rattenbury. Sure enough Rattenbury was found downstairs seriously injured, bludgeoned around the head with the mallet. Alma tried to revive him and got the housekeeper to call for the doctor.

Throughout the doctor's visit Alma was hysterical, drunk and non-committal about how this could have happened. When the police arrived at the Villa Madeira Alma said that her lover was responsible but subsequently changed her story and said that she had 'done him in' herself. After a few brief moments of trying to blame Rattenbury's son (who was not even in the country at that time) she reiterated that she was responsible. The following morning she was arrested for attempted murder.

Two days later, Stoner confessed to the housekeeper, Irene Riggs, that he had been responsible. The housekeeper was unsure of what to do with this information, feeling sure that Stoner would instantly deny his guilt if he was questioned by the police. Irene told the doctor who had attended to Rattenbury on the night of the attack and he, in turn, contacted the police. Stoner was arrested. Francis Rattenbury died of his injuries and consequently Stoner was charged with murder.

In fact Stoner seemed quite happy to take full responsibility. He spoke of how he had waited outside the French windows before attacking the sleeping Rattenbury. Meanwhile Alma remained adamant that it was she who would shoulder the blame for the murder. As the trial approached her stance slowly changed as she realised that it would be wrong to leave her children without a mother, and she came to the conclusion that she would plead not guilty.

Alma Rattenbury and George Stoner were tried together at the Old Bailey on 27 May 1935. Although Stoner refused to say anything at the trial the main mitigating circumstances put forward by Stoner's defence was that he was high on cocaine at the time of the murder, something which was almost certainly untrue. There was an instance some while back of him telling Alma that he had once used cocaine, but this seems an unlikely invention of his to make himself sound more sophisticated to his older lover. Certainly it seemed from the police interviews that Stoner was unfamiliar with the appearance of the drug or how it might be administered.

Four days later, a case that was now fascinating the whole nation was coming to a conclusion. The jury took just fifty minutes to reach their verdict. Stoner was found guilty of murder and sentenced to death while Alma was released. However, this was far from being the end of the case. Public sympathy was with the convicted Stoner, felt to have been led astray by a much older woman, and a haggard-looking Alma, by now both physically and mentally ill, was booed by a large crowd as she left the Old Bailey.

Alma initially stayed at a nephew's house and then at a nursing home. On Monday 3 June she took the train from Waterloo to Christchurch and walked across the meadows to the railway bridge, which spans a tributary of the River Avon. It was a place that Stoner had once mentioned to her. Alma wrote a couple of brief notes and then committed suicide. Most of her thoughts were about her children and their future but it is also clear that she genuinely loved Stoner, whom she believed was soon to be executed.

A petition containing 320,000 signatures, including those of the local mayor and MP, was later handed in to the Home Secretary. Stoner's sentence was commuted to penal servitude for life. In fact he was released after just seven years.

The Basingstoke Cornfield Tragedy

ON 14 AUGUST 1924 A COUPLE FROM LONDON WHO WERE WALKING BETWEEN BASINGSTOKE AND SHERBORNE ST JOHN SPOTTED A BODY LYING IN A NEARBY CORNFIELD. WHEN THE POLICE WERE CALLED THEY WERE ABLE TO IDENTIFY THE WOMAN, WHO HAD BEEN BEATEN TO DEATH, AS LUCY FISHER. SHE HAD BEEN MISSING FROM HOME SINCE THE PREVIOUS EVENING.

Lucy lived in Lancaster Road in Basingstoke; she was 42 years of age, married to a local leather worker and had three children. It seemed from neighbours that Lucy had become infatuated with William Matthews, a 24-year-old who lived just the other side of the railway line in nearby Queen's Road. She was seeing him on a regular basis under the pretence of going for a walk. It seems that Lucy's husband remained totally unaware of his wife's new romantic interest.

William Matthews had been discharged from the army and he now had a variety of casual jobs around Basingstoke which he supplemented with his work as a

Old postcard of Vyne Road in Sherborne St John close to the murder scene cc

part-time pianist. When questioned about the murder, Matthews admitted that he had been seeing Lucy but said that he had parted company with her that day in Vyne Road and had proceeded to go straight home, just as he had assumed Lucy had done. William's sister, Edith Matthews, was able to confirm that her brother had indeed come home in the way that he had described, but added that he had omitted to mention to the police that on arrival back in Queen's Road he had confessed to murder.

Superintendent Wyatt was the first to interview Matthews and the suspect did now concede that there had been friction between himself and Lucy regarding finance. He said, 'She'd been jawing me over money matters.' Matthews' clothes were submitted for analysis and sure enough just about every tested item was found

41

to have traces of blood. Matthews had little in the way of explanation, claiming that he was unable to remember what had happened. His statement did mention holding Lucy by the throat in retaliation for her grabbing him, but the rest of the encounter was a blank in his mind.

Matthews was duly charged with the murder of Lucy Fisher. Although it was only a short distance between the police station and the court, Matthews had to make the journey on foot, which gave the chance for large crowds to accumulate to gaze at the prisoner. Matthews had a hat pulled low over his face to try to conceal himself and once in court he hid his face beneath a handkerchief, sobbing throughout the short procedure to have him remanded in custody.

At the subsequent trial it emerged just how sick Matthews had become. He had been a private in the Royal Marines but had been invalided out with a mental illness in August 1918. Since then had been seriously ill with epilepsy and other neurological disorders. There was evidence of suicide bids and terrifying mood swings. The opinion of the doctors appointed by the court was that at the time of the ferocious attack on Lucy, Matthews had been out of control and unable to tell the difference between right and wrong. He was found guilty but insane. William Matthews was sentenced to be detained at His Majesty's pleasure.

The Melksham Murder

JOHN GURD WAS A WANTED MAN. IN APRIL 1892 HE HAD KILLED HENRY RICHARDS OF MELKSHAM. WITH THE POLICE CLOSING IN ON HIM, THE FUGITIVE WAS FINALLY SPOTTED CLOSE TO THE GATES OF LONGLEAT PARK. IN THE SCUFFLE THAT FOLLOWED GURD MANAGED TO FIRE TWO BULLETS, KILLING ONE OF THE ARRESTING OFFICERS.

John Gurd was born in 1861 close to Shaftesbury, where his father was an agricultural labourer. He joined the Royal Marines and it was at about this time that he adopted the name of Louis Hamilton. It was a pseudonym that he used sporadically throughout the remainder of his life. It seems that he served in both India and Africa before falling ill and being discharged on medical grounds. Having been invalided out of the army in 1890 he found employment at the Wiltshire County Asylum in Devizes.

While working at the asylum Gurd met a housemaid called Florence Adams. They became engaged but, with only days to go before the wedding, Florence called it off. Furious and heartbroken, Gurd quit his job and returned to live with his mother, believing that Florence's family must surely have poisoned her mind against him. Letters were sent by Gurd to Florence at this time professing his undying love for her but also a simmering hatred towards her family. Without Florence by his side he felt that he could not carry on alone and announced that he would shortly be leaving for America to start a new life.

On 8 April 1892, having failed to leave for the United States, Gurd arrived in Melksham hoping to track down Henry Richards. Henry was Florence's uncle and appears to have had no particular dislike of Florence's former fiancé, but nevertheless Gurd had it in his head that Henry was responsible for the failure of the relationship. Some reports said that Gurd waited for Richards outside a pub where he knew he was drinking and then attacked him. In fact the two men had enjoyed a perfectly friendly drink together. As they parted company and Richards started to walk home down Spa Road and over the canal bridge, Gurd exacted his revenge. He produced a revolver and shot Richards twice in the back, leaving him mortally wounded.

Although the murderer was quickly away from the scene of the crime, there had been witnesses to the shooting and so there was little doubt as to who had been responsible. The police were now able to swiftly mount a manhunt for John Gurd.

Over the next couple of days the wanted man was spotted a number of times in the area around Bath and Frome. Four days after the shooting Gurd had turned up outside the Royal Oak in Corsley. It was late at night and the fugitive was looking for board and lodging. The period on the run had taken its toll and he was dishevelled

The former Crown Inn, Market Place Melksham where Gurd and Richards had their final drink

© Nikki Rowe

and confused. When he was refused a bed for the night he shot one of the horses which was tethered outside belonging to one of the late-night drinkers. The police were called and, from the description given, deduced that it was the man wanted for the shooting of Henry Richards. Gurd was cornered and in the process of being arrested he shot dead Sergeant Enos Molden of the Wiltshire Constabulary.

The trial of John Gurd was held in Salisbury. People were now able to hear Florence's side of this tragic story. It seems that she broke off the engagement as she was shocked to hear that her fiancé was in the habit of borrowing money and that he now owed a lot of money to several of the patients at the asylum.

Gurd was to show some contrition for the shooting of the local policeman, and said that if he had just had a few moments more he would have killed himself instead of the arresting officer. However, he maintained that he was fully justified in killing Henry Richards.

As the trial went on it seemed that there was little possibility of Gurd being considered insane at the time of the shootings. Florence said that he always appeared steady, and she did not consider him a quick-tempered man. She always thought him to be in possession of his full senses. Gurd, on the other hand, said that he was only sorry that Florence wasn't with her uncle on the evening of the first shooting as he would have quite liked to have shot her too.

The jury returned in eight minutes and brought in a verdict of guilty and the judge sentenced him to death. As it turned out, as the date of his execution approached, Gurd's opinions did soften. The newspapers reported how the condemned man had expressed his desire to see Florence one last time. From the condemned cell Gurd wrote letters to his aunt in which he said that Florence had been to see him twice and there was some sort of reconciliation between the two of them. John Gurd was executed at Devizes prison on 26 July 1892.

The Salisbury Horror

ON SATURDAY 31 OCTOBER 1908, A TWELVE-YEAR-OLD BOY NAMED TEDDY HASKELL WAS MURDERED AT HIS HOME IN THE FISHERTON AREA OF SALISBURY. A FEW DAYS LATER, WHEN AN ARREST WAS MADE AND THE IDENTITY OF THE SUSPECT MADE KNOWN, PEOPLE WERE INCREDULOUS.

Following illness, at the age of six Teddy had one of his legs amputated. Despite this Teddy was said to be cheerful and popular and was well liked by everyone who knew him. He lived with his widowed 34-year-old mother, Flora at 40 Meadow Road. She was a laundress and, despite her low income, Flora was saving up to buy her son an artificial leg.

Around 10.30 on the night of the murder, a nephew of Mrs Haskell went to her house to return a shilling which he had borrowed. As he went to enter via the back door he became aware of various rustling and thumping noises and then the sound of Flora screaming. When she opened the door she was in a state of high anxiety and begged her nephew to track down the man who had just left, who had killed Teddy. But there was no one to be seen.

In the kerfuffle that followed the neighbours were alerted and medical help was summoned. While waiting for the police, one neighbour headed off in the direction indicated by Flora where the suspect was supposed to have gone. In York Road outside the Duke of York pub there were several possible suspects, but fearing for Flora's welfare he turned back to the house rather than investigate any further.

When neighbours and the police had gone upstairs, they found Teddy still in his bed but with his throat cut. A knife was lying at the bottom of the stairs near the kitchen. The drawer where Teddy's savings had been located was found to be broken open and some of the money had been taken.

Flora's account of the evening was that after putting Teddy to bed she had returned to the kitchen. She then heard a number of noises and, unsure where they were coming from, she went to the front door. An intruder then ran down the stairs and, pushing her out of the way, escaped. His parting shot was to toss the bloody knife in Flora's direction.

No one was able to confirm Flora's story and no one else saw anything of this intruder. Flora said that she had little more than a glimpse of the man and so her description was a little vague. The intruder was said to be between thirty and forty years of age, clean-shaven and dressed in a dark suit but no collar and tie, wearing a light-coloured cap. However, the police could find no trace of him then, or later.

On investigating the crime scene the police soon realised that the murder weapon was a knife belonging to Flora. Something about this incident was starting to feel not quite right. This development would have meant that the murderer had come into the house unarmed and then borrowed a knife. The alternative was that it was a botched robbery, in which case why was so little taken? Not even the entirety of Teddy's savings had been stolen.

Frank Richardson, the Chief Constable of Salisbury, now contacted London and the investigation which followed had the local constabulary being assisted by Inspector Walter Dew from Scotland Yard. Dew was becoming quite well known. He had been involved in the search for Jack the Ripper and later was to have more luck in capturing Harry the Valet, an international jewel thief involved in a particularly baffling robbery.

The newspapers were fascinated by the case and reported on the comings and goings of Chief Constable Richardson and Inspector Dew of Scotland Yard as they returned to the murder scene. It was to be Inspector Dew who insisted that Flora Haskell be charged with her son's murder.

Inspector Walter Dew of Scotland Yard, who wanted Flora Haskell to be charged with murder cc

The trial that followed was held in Devizes. The prosecution argued that Flora had killed her son in an attempt to deliver him from a life of suffering. The cheerful demeanour of Teddy and his mother made this seem a weak case. Any number of people attested to how well they were coping with the difficulties that they faced.

While the motive may have been difficult for the prosecution to establish, some of the evidence was quite compelling. For instance, why did Flora not immediately rush upstairs to check on Teddy rather than saying, on more than one occasion, that he had been murdered, at a time when she had no proof that this was so? Mrs Haskell also had a bloodstained handkerchief in her possession, although she claimed this was the result of a nosebleed. Medical experts also testified that the pattern of the bloodstains suggested that it was unlikely that the knife could have been thrown at Flora. A far more likely explanation was that it had simply been left in the place where it was found.

In their deliberations the jury remained deadlocked. A good deal of the evidence seemed to point towards Flora being guilty, but she was hard-working and respectable, and surely she would not have killed a child to whom she was clearly devoted. A retrial was ordered.

At this second trial, again held in Devizes, Flora's sister-in-law appeared as an additional witness. Her evidence did little to advance the defendant's case as she spoke of Flora's intention to marry again and the fact that Flora had temporarily borrowed money from Teddy's savings, in order to pay the rent. So it was now apparent that there had been a marriage proposal which Mrs Haskell had been mulling over. It seems that this was from Alfred John Mold, a seafarer. While he was away at sea at the time of the murder, and clearly not implicated in the incident, he may still hold the key to the case. Perhaps Teddy was seen as an impediment to Flora being able to move on with her life.

Flora herself did not give evidence at the trials. As it seems likely that she would have made a good impression on the jury it seems a surprising step by the defence. Perhaps the fear was that cross-examination may have exposed a slightly forgetful side to her nature. After all, one of her comments at an earlier interview had been, 'If I did it … I don't remember.'

The retrial was concluded on 3 April 1909. The jury took eighty minutes to come to a verdict of not guilty. Inspector Dew always believed Flora Haskell to be responsible and regretted that they had failed to secure her conviction. It was a disappointment that must have been tempered by his celebrated apprehension of Dr Crippen a couple of years later. As for Flora Haskell, after she was released she moved to London, where she died of tuberculosis in 1920.

The Gussage Murder

ALTHOUGH HE WAS MARRIED, WILLIAM BURTON WAS HAVING AN AFFAIR WITH WINIFRED MITCHELL, A YOUNGER WOMAN WHO WORKED AT THE SAME FARM. WINIFRED IMAGINED A NEW LIFE FOR THEM BOTH IN CANADA, WHEREAS BURTON'S THOUGHTS WERE OF MURDER.

In the spring of 1913 Burton was living in Gussage St Michael, a small rural village in East Dorset between Blandford Forum and Salisbury. He worked as a rabbit trapper on the nearby Manor Farm and, although married to a schoolteacher, it is said that he had a reputation for pursuing the local girls.

Inevitably Burton showed an interest in 24-year-old Winifred Mitchell, who had been appointed as the cook on the farm where she now lived and where Burton worked. Soon they became lovers. They aimed to keep the affair secret and certainly Winifred's family, back in the village, seemed oblivious to her liaison with a married man. However, the relationship was well known amongst the other servants at the house and at least one of their work colleagues was involved in passing letters between the two of them.

It was not long before Burton wanted to end the affair. One possible scenario is that Winifred got tired of his promises to leave his wife and so gave him an ultimatum. Burton, realising that he was in trouble, tried to break off the relationship but Winifred was having none of it and threatened to tell his wife. There also seems to be a belief that Winifred was pregnant. In fact she was not expecting a child and it is only conjecture that this had any part in the matters reaching a head. Nevertheless, whatever the reason, a plan was now hatched.

Burton told Winifred that they would shortly be leaving for a new life in Canada but that she was to tell her friends that she was going to London. The two of them met on the agreed night, Winifred thinking they were off to enjoy a new life abroad. She arrived by bicycle at the spot close to where her lover had supposedly arranged for a car to come and meet them and whisk them away to a new life overseas. In fact Burton now murdered his lover, disposing of the body in a shallow grave that he had already dug.

On one of Winifred's previous visits to her family she had announced that she would be leaving to work for a lady in London, which was exactly what Burton had wanted her to tell everyone. Initially her parents had accepted this career advancement at face value but on reflection they must have had some suspicions that all was not as it seemed. Within a few days Winifred's parents visited the police saying that they feared that their daughter was in trouble and probably not in London at all.

While all this was unfolding, Burton was still at the farm keeping up appearances and behaving as if the disappearance of Winnie was nothing to do with him. But then, a week after Winnie vanished, a fellow worker from the Manor found a dental plate with three false teeth when walking across Sovel Plantation. This part of the farm was regularly used by Burton for his rabbiting activities and he must have been quaking in his boots that his actions were about to be uncovered.

For some weeks the police were in possession of the teeth but little else to help track down Winnie. Burton seemed to be in the clear until, on 2 May 1913, several weeks after she was last seen, Winifred's body was discovered by some children while out playing and exploring. She had been killed by a wound to the head which, as the inquest soon revealed, had been inflicted by a shotgun from a distance of no more than four feet.

In addition to the grave being located in an area which Burton was known to visit on a daily basis there was soon the incriminating testimony of Leonard Mitcham, who was the son of the village carpenter. Leonard said that he lent William his father's gun on 31 March. It had been safely returned, but it was clear that some of the cartridges had been used.

There also seems to be a fair amount of conjecture concerning Winifred's bicycle. It initially disappeared at the same time as its owner, but was to subsequently turn up close to her family's house. It was found leaning against an apple tree and nearby there were the

Dorchester Prison, now closed for redevelopment, where William Burton was executed for murder on 24 June 1913

footprints of a man who had been wearing heavy boots. It seems that the presence of the bicycle had not been factored into Burton's plan to escape from the murder scene and, in the absence of any other ideas, he had simply wheeled it back to her parents' house.

The two-day trial was held on 3 and 4 June 1913, at Dorset Assizes in Dorchester. One fact emerging at the trial was that the lovers' supposed rendezvous and trip to Canada had been planned for a few days earlier but had to be abandoned due to Winnie's last-minute indecision. An interesting point, although it was not particularly investigated at the trial, was the fact that on the date of the original elopement Burton would have not have been in possession of Leonard's gun. Nevertheless there could be little doubt about the identity of the murderer and after just a few minutes of deliberation the jury concluded that Winifred had been murdered by Burton.

Prior to his execution Burton was visited by his mother, wife and son in the condemned cell. It is reported in the newspapers that he made a full confession.

The Murder at Broadwindsor

JOHN AND MARTHA BROWN WERE MARRIED ON 24 JANUARY 1852 AT THE REGISTRY OFFICE AT WAREHAM. MARTHA WAS 41 YEARS OF AGE AT THIS TIME, WHILE JOHN WAS TWENTY YEARS YOUNGER. FOUR YEARS LATER SHE WAS TO BE EXECUTED FOR HIS MURDER.

Martha had been married before; some years earlier she had married a widower who worked as a butcher. This marriage also involved a significant age difference as he was twenty years older than herself. However, unlike her second marriage, this had by all accounts been a happy union.

John Brown had a reputation as something of a philanderer and had recently been caught by Martha in a compromising situation with Mary, the wife of a neighbour called William Davis. Despite a huge argument the marriage limped on for a while, although the strain was about to reach breaking point.

On one occasion John arrived home at 2am to be accused by Martha of being out with Mary Davis again.

He denied this and said he had just been out for a couple of drinks and a game of skittles. A violent argument followed which culminated in John lying dead on the floor. Martha ran down the road to a neighbour's house saying that John had been killed by a kick from a horse. The police were called and despite claiming her innocence Martha was arrested on 5 July 1856 for the murder of her husband.

The inquest was held on Monday 7 July 1856 at 5pm in the Rose and Crown Inn. Here it was revealed that John had received six wounds to his head, and all the evidence pointed to the deed being committed in the room where he had been found. It was thought that death was instantaneous. The inquest returned a verdict of murder and while Martha was not named as the murderer, she was soon packed off to Dorchester Gaol to await her trial for murder.

The trial took place at the Crown Court in Dorchester on 21 July 1856. It lasted just one day but went on until 10pm. Martha pleaded not guilty to the charge of murder. The defence was based on the purely circumstantial nature of the evidence against her, as well as her previous good character. Martha's previous employer was brought to court to explain that she had worked for him for ten years and he found her kind and inoffensive and surely incapable of such a violent act. It seems that there was no blood to be found on her clothes, and the fact that

The Old Crown Court at Dorchester located at Shire Hall and the scene of the trial of Martha Brown

there had been a great deal of force used against her husband left a question mark over whether she would have been powerful enough to inflict the wounds.

The horse explanation had been widely discredited and there were now efforts to distance Martha from this version of events. The new account was that she had not witnessed the kick by the horse, but the mortally injured John had muttered something about it before succumbing to his injuries. However, the scene of the crime did not seem to support the story as there was no blood in the yard or road where the kicking incident was supposed to have occurred, and no evidence of Martha having dragged the body into the house. Another new version of events

TThe Rose and Crown in Birdsmoorgate where the inquest took place. It is no longer a pub

appeared involving the first visitors to the house simply surmising that a kick from a horse must be involved and Martha subsequently repeating their words.

The jury retired at six o'clock and did not return for four hours, but when they did it was to give the verdict of guilty. Martha was returned to Dorchester Gaol to await her execution.

Two days before her execution Martha finally described to the prison governor exactly what had happened to cause her husband's death. When she asked John not to see Mary again he lost his temper and the two of them quarrelled until the early hours of the morning without resolving anything. In the course of their arguments

61

John struck her a severe blow to the side of the head and thrashed her with a horsewhip. Martha was in great pain and as soon as she got the opportunity she picked up a hatchet, which was used for breaking coal and was lying close by, and struck him several blows to the head.

While there was a genuine wave of sympathy for Martha, who was trapped in an abusive relationship, attempts to get her a reprieve ultimately failed. She was hanged on 9 August 1856.

The Fordingbridge Murder

IT WAS FOUR O'CLOCK IN THE AFTERNOON ON 22 JUNE 1862 WHEN A LABOURER, 29-YEAR-OLD GEORGE GILBERT FROM FROG LANE IN FORDINGBRIDGE, WENT TO FIND THE LOCAL POLICEMAN. HE HAD SEEN A PARASOL BLOWING AROUND IN A FIELD AND WHEN HE INVESTIGATED HE REALISED THAT THERE HAD BEEN A SHOCKING ATTACK ON A YOUNG WOMAN.

Old postcard of Vyne Road in Sherborne St John close to the murder scene cc

The story that Gilbert related was that he had returned home to where he lodged with his half-brother Charles Philpot carrying the parasol. His sister-in-law had told Gilbert to go to the police immediately. Gilbert had done so and he now led a small party to where he had found the body. The woman had been attacked, partially strangled and then drowned in ditch water.

The body was identified as that of Mary Hall. She was 23 years of age, and had lived with her father and stepmother at Midgham Farm situated close to Fordingbridge. She was a member of the congregation at her local church and that Sunday morning she had set off along her usual route, which was a footpath close to the river, a journey of about a mile, to attend the church service. She might have been expected home at lunchtime but when she did not turn up her family assumed that Mary must have met up with some of her cousins (she was in fact engaged to be married to one of them) and was probably having dinner with them.

The inquest was held at the Greyhound Inn in Salisbury Street in Fordingbridge. Gilbert told the coroner that he knew nothing about the incident other than that he was the one who had discovered the body. His account convinced no one. After an inquest lasting six hours, a verdict of wilful murder against Gilbert was recorded and he was sent to stand trial.

It seems that Gilbert was known to the Hall family, partly for the work he had done at the farm at various times in his life, and partly for the unwanted attentions that he had paid to Mary in the past. He was also pretty well known to the police as he had a long string of convictions. Some were comparatively trivial and related to poaching but there were also convictions for burglary and highway robbery. He had served sentences at Portland Prison, Millbank, Pentonville and the *Stirling Castle*, a prison hulk moored at Portsmouth.

Gilbert's trial began in Winchester on 19 July 1862 and the courtroom was completely packed out. Given the nature of the crime that Gilbert was suspected of committing, most people had expected him to resemble a monster. In fact the newspapers reported that he was quite small (his prison records put him at five feet and two inches) and rather studious in appearance. Throughout his trial he behaved very respectfully towards the court.

The defence stressed that Gilbert had done little to disguise his obvious involvement in the case; after all he had found the body. They felt that his behaviour had been exactly how an innocent man might behave. He was aware that something was wrong in the area around the ditch (partly due to the parasol and partly because the cattle seemed to be in a disturbed state) and when he investigated he had found the body. Surely, the defence asserted, if he were the murderer he would not be so foolish as to implicate himself by going directly to the police.

The prosecution pointed out that from the spot where Gilbert claimed to have retrieved the parasol Mary's body simply could not have been seen, which is what he had claimed. One of his friends, John Turner, spoke of his fixation on Mary and how he had engineered occasions when he would bump into her on the footpath. Further testimony placed Gilbert on and around the footpath at various times throughout the day. Witnesses spoke of blood spots on his waistcoat, while his clothes in general were covered in mud from the ditch where Mary was found.

It took the jury less than twenty-five minutes to return their verdict of guilty. A crowd of 10,000 people attended the execution of George Gilbert at Winchester Prison on 4 August 1862.

Death of a Dorset Cowman

CHARLOTTE MCHUGH WAS BORN IN LONDONDERRY, NORTHERN IRELAND, IN 1904. AT THE AGE OF EIGHTEEN SHE FELL IN LOVE WITH FREDERICK BRYANT FROM SHERBORNE. THE STORY SEEMS TO BE QUITE A ROMANTIC ONE: SHE WAS A LOCAL CATHOLIC GIRL AND HE WAS A PROTESTANT SERVING IN THE BRITISH ARMY. HOWEVER, IT WAS TO END IN MURDER.

Frederick's father had been a carter on a farm in Poyntington and from the time that Frederick was barely in his teens he had been assisting with the cattle on the same farm. After serving his time in the Dorset Regiment, Frederick returned to England with his new love, Charlotte. They married a little while later at Wells in Somerset and initially lived briefly in Frome. Frederick resumed civilian life as a farm labourer and by 1925 was working as a cowman at a farm near Yeovil.

By the end of 1933 Charlotte had met and embarked on an affair with a horse trader called Leonard Parsons. In 1934 Charlotte and Frederick moved to the village of Coombe, where again Frederick found employment as a farm labourer. The move seems to have had little impact on their domestic arrangements as curiously Parsons simply moved in with them and his affair with Charlotte continued unabated.

Clearly, at least for some of the time, Frederick did not seem too worried about Charlotte's infidelity. Initially Parsons and Frederick Bryant appeared to get on quite well and drank together in the local pub, the Crown. Parsons did not live with the Bryants on a permanent basis but rather stayed there between business trips. After all, he also had a common-law wife, Priscilla Loveridge, with whom he had fathered four children.

It seems that eventually Frederick's patience reached breaking point. He could stand the situation no longer and ordered his wife's lover to leave. Parsons duly left, but taking Charlotte with him, and headed for Dorchester where they rented rooms. It proved to be a temporary arrangement and soon the three were reunited once again at the Bryants' house in this loose and uneasy arrangement.

In May 1935, immediately after eating the lunch that Charlotte had cooked, Frederick was taken ill with severe stomach pains. The doctor came to see him and diagnosed gastroenteritis. The illness passed and after a few days Frederick was able to return to work. Over the next six months there were three further bouts of illness but on each occasion he recovered.

Throughout this period Parsons had almost entirely disappeared off the scene. He was supposedly looking for work elsewhere, but it seems probable that his passion for Charlotte had by now all but disappeared. With the house somewhat emptier than of late Charlotte moved a widowed friend of hers named Lucy Ostler into her home. Lucy was to witness Frederick's final attack of illness on the night of 22 December 1935. Once again it was the stomach pains but this time it was so bad that he was admitted to the hospital in Sherborne, where he died the following afternoon.

At the post-mortem the pathologist found an excessive amount of arsenic in Frederick's body. The findings were reported to Dorset Constabulary and Charlotte was removed to the workhouse in Sturminster Newton while further tests were carried out, interviews were conducted and the house was searched.

Although it felt like it would be only a matter of time before the inevitable happened, it was not until 10 February 1936 that Charlotte was arrested and charged with the murder of her husband. At Charlotte's trial, three months later, Lucy's evidence was particularly damning as she related how she would read to the illiterate Charlotte from the newspaper. She firmly recalled reading aloud the details of a murder case and Charlotte's particular interest in the poison used, which was arsenic. Lucy also told the court that on the night

Charlotte Bryant at the time of her trial © Bill Walden

before Frederick died, Charlotte had made him an Oxo drink and that he was violently sick after taking it.

The testimony of Charlotte's eldest two children was particularly damaging to their mother's case. It is difficult to see how it all fits into the bigger picture but Ernest, her older son, related how she had asked him to dispose of some blue bottles at about the time of the fatal poisoning. Her daughter, Lily, told how she had seen Parsons with a blue bottle whose contents had fizzed when poured onto a stone by Parsons in front of Charlotte. An empty tin of weedkiller, which was in poor condition following an attempt to burn it, was also damning evidence as this too contained a strong presence of arsenic. Charlotte denied knowing about poison or possessing any weedkiller.

Despite the fact that Charlotte acquitted herself well in the dock, the jury deliberated for barely an hour before returning a verdict of guilty. She spent almost six weeks in the condemned cell where she decided, after much agonising, against seeing her children as she felt it would be too painful for them. Despite strenuous efforts being made to have the sentence commuted to life imprisonment, there was to be no intervention and on 15 July 1936 Charlotte Bryant was hanged at Exeter Prison.

The Swindon Widow's Murder

BETWEEN SEPTEMBER 1938 AND THE FOLLOWING JANUARY RALPH SMITH HAD BEEN LODGING AT THE HOUSE OF BEATRICE BAXTER AT 63 ARGYLE STREET IN SWINDON. A RELATIONSHIP DEVELOPED BETWEEN THE TWO OF THEM, BUT ON 4 MARCH 1939 THIS CAME TO A SHOCKING AND VIOLENT END.

Beatrice Delia Kimble was born in Highworth, a short distance north-east of Swindon, where her father had been an engine fitter's labourer. By 1901 Beatrice was working as a domestic servant, and the family was living in Haydon Street in Swindon. In 1908 Beatrice married William Baxter and before long they moved in with William's parents in Avening Street, Gorse Hill along with their own two children. William worked for the Great Western Railway, and the two of them were known to be keen cyclists.

Following William's death in 1936, to make ends meet Beatrice let out rooms in the family house in Argyle Street, where they had now moved. One of the rooms was let out to Ralph Smith, a native of West Hartlepool who had been a locomotive fireman, a steelworker and, more recently, in the employ of the Swindon gasworks.

Soon a relationship developed between landlady and lodger but there was a problem: Smith became very jealous of Beatrice, who had an outgoing personality and enjoyed the company of other men. On 10 January 1939 Beatrice called the police after an altercation with Smith had left her bleeding from the mouth. They calmed the situation and Beatrice allowed Smith to stay the night on the grounds that he had nowhere to go, provided that he left the next morning, which he did.

Smith did not contact Beatrice again until 4 March, and it subsequently emerged that much of the intervening time Smith had spent in Bristol. Now back in Swindon he approached his old lodgings where he saw Beatrice just leaving in order to attend a dance. He asked her to take him back, which she refused. Smith, now overcome with a jealous rage, drew an open razor and attacked her.

A woman who was passing heard the screams. She went to Beatrice's assistance and found that she had received a serious wound to the neck. She was able to help her to her home and a doctor and the police were sent for. Mrs Baxter was removed to hospital but died shortly after admission.

It seemed that Smith had no particular intention of staging a getaway. Shortly after the attack he walked into Gorse Hill Police Station and made a statement that he had been responsible. He was arrested and charged with murder.

The empty Gloucester Prison today. The wall to the right of the arched window is where the old hanging shed stood. There was internal access from the condemned cell

© Bill Walden

The trial took place at the Old Bailey on 3 May 1939. Part of Smith's defence was that Beatrice really should have survived the attack. Certainly the medical evidence produced did support the theory that if the wound had been attended to swiftly there was every chance that she might have lived. Unfortunately no expert assistance had been close at hand.

The other line of defence was that Smith had suffered a brain injury in an accident at work some eighteen months before the murder. Police investigations of this alleged accident at the steelworks turned up nothing and therefore the prosecution claimed that it was simply a ruse to escape the death penalty. Smith was found guilty of Beatrice's murder. He was transferred to the condemned cell at Gloucester prison and on Wednesday 7 June 1939 he became the last man to be hanged there.

The Chine Murder

WHILE WALKING ALONG THE BOURNEMOUTH PROMENADE ON 3 JULY 1946, DOREEN MARSHALL MET AN RAF OFFICER, GROUP CAPTAIN RUPERT BROOK. SHE ACCEPTED BROOK'S INVITATION TO TAKE AFTERNOON TEA AT HIS HOTEL, THE TOLLARD ROYAL ON THE WEST CLIFF. LATER THEY ALSO AGREED TO DINE TOGETHER. LATE THAT NIGHT BROOK SAID THAT HE WOULD WALK DOREEN BACK TO HER OWN HOTEL. THIS WAS THE LAST TIME THAT SHE WAS SEEN ALIVE.

Doreen Margaret Marshall was born in Brentford in 1924. She had served with the WRNS during the war and had been discharged in the summer of 1946. She had recently suffered from the flu and measles and had taken a holiday in Bournemouth to recover. Throughout the war many of the Bournemouth hotels had been taken over for use by the armed forces but the Norfolk was open for business as usual and it was here that Doreen stayed.

It seems that after dinner, Brook took Doreen to the hotel lounge of the Tollard Royal to listen to dance music on the wireless. Despite the fact that Brook was good-looking and well-spoken, Marshall was becoming increasingly uncomfortable with her dinner companion,

The Norfolk Hotel where Doreen Marshall was staying at the time of her murder cc

and asked another guest to call a taxi for her, claiming that she was tired. But Brook cancelled the taxi and offered to walk her home.

The next morning, when no sign of Doreen was found at the Norfolk Hotel, the manager contacted his counterpart at the Tollard Royal, as he knew she had dined there. The manager was able to report that the RAF officer was there but there was no clue as to the whereabouts of Doreen. On Saturday 6 July, realising that he was clearly implicated in the disappearance, Brook duly telephoned Bournemouth Police Station to see if he could offer any assistance. He confirmed that he had dined with Doreen Marshall, but said he had left her in the gardens in central Bournemouth and had no further clue to her whereabouts.

Doreen's family now travelled down to Bournemouth and when they arrived at the Police Station, Brook was even introduced to them. He joked to them about his similarity to the wanted poster of the murderer Neville Heath, who was at large at that time. Indeed there was a clear resemblance, and this was largely due to the fact that Heath and Brook were in fact one and the same man. Doreen had become the latest victim of one of the most notorious murderers in the history of British crime.

Neville Heath was now 29 years of age, He had at one point been in the RAF but was dismissed for stealing a car and going absent without leave. Other crimes included obtaining credit by fraud, housebreaking and forgery. More recently he had also spent some time in the South African Air Force. On returning to Britain in 1946 Heath took a room at a Notting Hill hotel where he met and murdered Margery Gardner. By the time that the body was discovered Heath was on his way to Worthing and subsequently on to Bournemouth and his fateful meeting with Doreen.

In the woods at Branksome Dene Chine on the evening of 7 July, dog walker Kathleen Evans of Pinewood Road saw a swarm of flies above a rhododendron thicket. She used a telephone kiosk to contact the police, who then set about the grim task of recovering Doreen's body. It was increasingly clear that Heath (still using the alias of Brook) was involved in the crime. A left-luggage ticket for Bournemouth Station was found in his possession and when the items were retrieved they firmly implicated him in the murder of Doreen. Further evidence came from a pawnbroker in Parkstone Avenue who clearly recognised Heath from his visit and his attempt to pawn Doreen's diamond ring.

Heath was questioned again, and now he admitted his real identity. The next day he was transferred to London where he was charged with the earlier murder of Margery Gardner. The trial of Neville Heath began on 24 September 1946. Heath at first spoke of how he had lent the Notting Hill hotel room to a man called Jack who was surely the murderer, but this feeble explanation was quickly abandoned under the weight of evidence. Heath originally instructed his counsel to plead guilty, but there was a change of heart when it was thought he could be found insane and possibly evade the death penalty. The murders of the women and his lacklustre attempts at covering his tracks and even his trip to the police station would perhaps be enough to indicate that he was not in his right mind.

Expert witnesses testified that the accused knew what he was doing, but not that it was wrong. They confirmed that in their conversations with Heath he showed no remorse, nor any appreciation of what any other people would think of his behaviour. However, in the courtroom the prosecution were able to run rings around the expert

Neville Heath cc

witnesses whose responses regarding Heath's mental state at the time of the murder sounded naive and unconvincing.

There certainly seemed to be signs that Heath knew that his actions were wrong. When he was at the Tollard Royal Hotel he had changed rooms (from room 71 to 81) in order to have one that contained a gas fire. With it being summer he surely was not feeling the cold and it was thought to be evidence that he had contemplated gassing himself in revulsion at his own actions. It was certainly a possibility as there was also an unposted note to his parents which stated his intention to end his own life.

Heath was found guilty and sentenced to death by hanging. He occupied himself as he awaited his execution by composing a series of perfectly lucid and well-written letters. While he had refused to see anyone from his family, in the final note written to his parents he stated that 'My only regret at leaving the world, is that I have been damned unworthy of you both.' He was executed on 16 October 1946 at Pentonville Prison.